iddlestixs opened its doors in historic Lafayette, NJ in July 2010, inspired completely from my publication: Piddlestixs.

Housed in a former turn of the century theater and WWI weigh, Piddlestixs tries to stay true to the magic and enchantment of

art, carnival and storybook fantasy.

Everything from vintage to new, dolls to circus toys, party wares, artful supplies, handmade, books, clothes, jewelry, gourmet treats, teas and the ecclectic OOAK's.

Valentina's Flying Parade

Meet Valentina Candyswirl from Glitterwoods. She is the winner of this years annual: Glitterwood Pagaent. Here she is on her glittery flying float!

Materials:

- Teardrop shape ornament
- Holiday bulb or ornate shape
- Authentic crinkle wire or boullion
- Tinsel and chenille stems
- Charlotte/cupie doll, Lisa Kettell Designs
- Dresden trims
- Crepe paper
- Millinery flowers, stamens and stems
- Glues: hot glue, craft glue of choice
- Tools: hot glue gun, scissors

Directions:

1. Attach teardrop ornament and holiday bulb ornament to each other using chenille stems in color of choice, by wrapping one end of the chenille stem ends around the bulb ornament opening and then one end of the teardrop ornament, repeat at other end of the teardrop shape, secure in place with hot glue.

2. Decorate your charlotte doll w/crepe paper, trim and millinery. Attach your doll to center of the teardrop shape using hot glue.

3. Now unravel crinkle wire or boullion and randomly wrap around the whole ornament.

4. Finish decorating your piece with more millinery, tinsel and trim.

Tips/Tricks:

- Use vintage images in place of the charlotte doll.
- Replace the crepe paper on the doll with ribbon, folded ephemera, or paper rosettes.
- Add paper rosettes to your piece, use discarded holiday garland light bulbs as crowns.
- Unravel a tin dish scrub in place of crinkle wire.

The picture on the left is an upclose view of the project. The image on the right is a picture of a variation of this project.

For more project ideas visit: faerieenchantment.blogspot.com

Enter The Sweet Shoppe
By: Marfi Bradford

Material List

Sweet Shoppe Box
- Cigar box
- Small cardboard cone
- Small wooden blocks (old 'Jenga' pieces work well)
- Wood dowel
- Toothpicks
- Foam hearts
- Assorted 'sweet' stickers and erasers
- Assorted rhinestones and beads
- Pink tag board
- Silver tinsel, fringe and trim
- Pink wool roving
- Acrylic paint: pink, blue
- Glitter
- Glue: white glue and glue sticks
- Tools: scissors, paint brush, glue gun

Sweet Shoppe Doll
- Carnival Lulu Doll, Lisa Kettell Designs
- Small tiara
- Sheet music
- Crepe paper: white
- Cake sticker
- Acrylic paints: dark pink, light pink, peach, white, red, light brown,
- Silver glitter glue

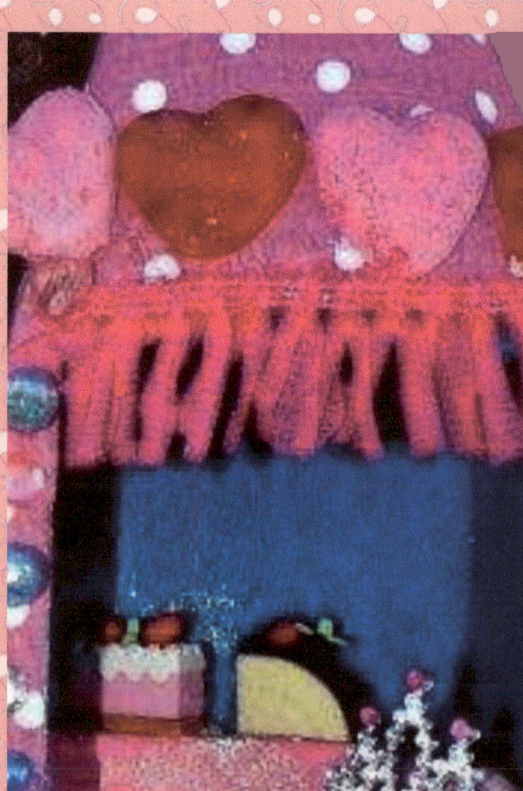

Optional: If you don't have a cigar box handy, try a wooden craft box, shoe box or jewelry box.

Directions

Sweet Shoppe

1. Paint inside of cigar box blue, glue cardboard cone to top. Drape material over, glue into place, pinching along the bottom to create folds.
2. Cut out material along the front of the box for doorway.
3. Paint wooden blocks pink and glue to inside of box.
4. Glue fringe trim and foam hearts over 'doorway', then drizzle hot glue on floor of box and arrange wool roving over it.
5. Add 'sweet' stickers and erasers to blocks inside, brush with white glue cover with glitter, glue rhinestones and beads to sides.
6. Cut out pennant and small sign out of tag board, attach pennant to toothpick and glue to top of cone.
7. Paint dowel red, write '5 cents each' on sign glue together and add to inside of box. Add glitter to foam hearts and pennant. Add silver tinsel to bottom front, glue Lulu into place.
8. Print out 'Sweet Shoppe' then cut out and attach to front of cone.

Sweet Shoppe Doll

1. Paint Carnival Lulu doll hair pink, cover in glitter.
2. Paint face and arms peach, add details to face with light brown for eye and nose, red for lips and cheeks, then paint pink and blue stripes on legs.

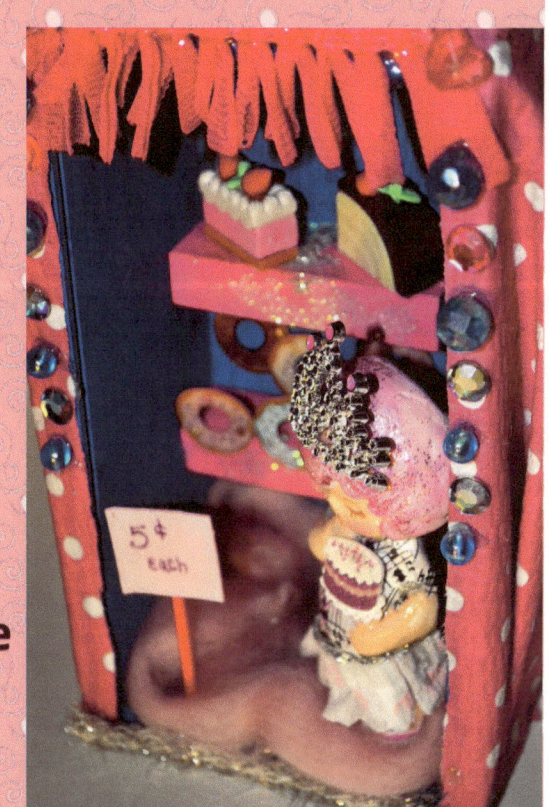

3. Using white glue, affix small bits of sheet music to torso for shirt, use silver glitter paint on collar and sleeves.
4. Paint pink polka dots onto crepe paper with a pencil eraser. Now add to doll for skirt, put silver glitter glue on waist and on feet for shoes.
5. Add cake sticker and tiara to the doll.

To see more of Marfi's works visit her blog at:
www.marfibradford.blogspot.com

Valentine ATC's

Materials
- Variety of scrapbook papers
- 3 1/2 by 2 1/2 inch piece of chip or matte board
- Small decorative chip board pieces
- Kewpie Magic and Cocoa Kewpie pieces, Lisa Kettell Designs
- Printed wording
- Millinery
- Tinsel, chenille stems
- Raffia
- German glass glitter or glitter of choice
- Glues: hot glue, craft glue, glue stick
- Tools: hot glue gun, scissors

Directions
1. Layer scrapbook paper over 3 1/2 by 2 1/2 piece of chip board, secure in place with glue stick, trim off excess paper.
2. Roll a tiny cone shape from scrapbook paper, hold in place with hot glue, attach to center of chipboard base.
3. Insert raffia or shredded paper into the tiny cone shape, attach the Kewpie doll. Decorate the cone and Kewpie doll with millinery, trim, glitter, wording and rosette.
4. Finish decorating your piece with more chipboard accents, millinery, glitter and trim.

Tips/Tricks
- Instead of a chipboard base try playing cards, balsa wood or masonite.
- To make a cone, draw a square shape, cut in 1/2 diagnol path, it will form a triangle. Roll each end together, glue in place.
- For more project ideas pick up my book: Altered Art Circus.

Artist Gallery

A Composer and A Circus Act is a piece created by Marfi Bradford's daughter Gabriella, who used the fractured doll part from Lisa Kettell Designs and inspiration from the book Altered Art Circus, Lisa Kettell I just love this!

The Alice Tin Assemblage to the right and the Sweet Doll Layout om the bottom were created by Deb Famularo using the kewpie doll and pixie party stix from Lisa Kettell Designs. I love love love these.

Antiquing in Andover
125 Main St, Andover, NJ 07821

Back in the summer, my friend Wanda Restrick invited me to stop by Made in the Shade to see her space, she had just added some new finds and wanted to give me some bags of vintage doilies and trims. So on the way to my own store, I picked up Mom and we headed over to Andover to see Wanda. Andover is about 8 miles from Lafayette where my store is located, both area's are filled with quaint antique stores and shops, perfect for the treasure hunter on a vintage exploration, what's equally amazing are the turn of the century structures and Victorians that these stores are in.

Made in the Shade is located in the heart of the Andover Antiques District and a perfect stop off for some treasures, including the Italian bistro located across the street in a Bed and Breakfast, the cheesecake is amazing.

From top to bottom Made in the Shade had some unique finds, but when I entered Wanda's space I fell over with joy, the whole space was filled with unique vintage finds, French frou frou and sweet 40's and 50's prom dresses, there was a pink one I was swooning over. In addition one could find gilded rococo framed prints and chandeliers. Made in the Shade is also known for their up-cycled and re-finished light fixtures which appeal to collectors of all kinds.

When Wanda has new stock, its time to rush over, we share the same tastes and love for vintage, after I finished exploring her space and the store, which I purchased some cute vintage dolls, figurines, cigar box, circus toys, postcards, 1800's books, including one on St.Theresa which I gave to my mom, a huge fan of hers, I gathered the huge bags of gorgeous doilies and trims, bided Wanda and the ladies farewell, headed through the picturesque back roads to my store, so that I could un-ravel and reflect on my beautiful and vintage morning spent with Wanda at Made in the Shade.

Sally Lunns was started over 30 years ago in Winter Haven, Florida, which eventually moved to Chester, NJ in 1983 and has been there ever since, with a recent 2nd location in Chatham, NJ which opened September 2010.

Sally Lunns was created from the creative minds of Theresa Gaffney and Jean Gaffney, a mother daughter team, who together built the Sally Lunns tradition of English tea in the US. Known for their scones and chicken pot pie, NJ residents have been coming back time after time to enjoy Sally Lunn's famous delicacies and create a tradition of their own.

Sinfully delectable scones, clotted cream, bread/butter pudding and Lemon Lavender Cake are just some of the favorites of Sally Lunn's customers and the creation of Theresa Gaffney, who along with Sally Lunns of Chatham, recently appeared on the food network in February 2011, showing viewers some sweet techniques.

The Gaffney Family has been in the restaurant/catering business for decades, with two famous restaurants in England, one in Covent Garden where they also sold antiques. After tiring from the whole sole idea of just restaurant catering, Theresa and Jean decided to focus on selling antiques from Europe in the US, by opening a 5,000 square foot store filled w/British Antiques in Winter Haven, where they hosted auctions every week, then after some thought, the Gaffney's decided to add teas, which they found to be more successful then the antiques themselves, eventually they merged the two concepts together bringing the old with the new to form the tradition of Sally Lunn's by serving afternoon tea within an antique world.

Sally Lunn's Tea Rooms are located in Chester, NJ and Chatham, NJ, both open Tuesday through Sunday 10:30-6:00pm, Monday's closed. In addition to a fabulous tea and lunch menu, Sally Lunns also offers Afternoon tea, Victorian high tea and a sweet Creamed tea, that are all inclusive tea packages for the serious tea room goer.

For more information, to book a party, get directions or to purchase one of their many packaged teas visit: www.sallylunns.com or friend them on Facebook.

The Queen of Hearts, had some tarts.......-Alice in Wonderland

EASY PETITS FOURS

Bake our white cake mix in jelly roll pan, 15½x10½x1 inch, as directed on package. Cool. Cut cake into small squares, rounds, diamonds, hearts or other shapes.

Place cake pieces upside down, a few at a time, on wire rack over large bowl. Pour Petits Fours Icing (below) over top so entire cake piece is covered at one time. Icing that drips off cake into bowl can be reheated and used again.

Decorate tops of cakes with silver dragées or Decorators' Icing: Mix 2 cups confectioners' sugar and enough hot water for consistency to be used in decorators' tube. Tint with few drops food color. **About thirty-five 2-inch squares.**

Petits Fours Icing

9 cups confectioners' sugar (about 2 pounds)
½ cup water
½ cup light corn syrup
1 teaspoon vanilla
½ teaspoon almond extract

In top of double boiler, mix all ingredients; heat over boiling water just to lukewarm. Remove from heat. Leave icing over hot water to keep it thin; tint with food color if you wish. If necessary, add hot water, a few drops at a time, until of spreading consistency.

Silhouette Cabinet Project

By: Lisa Kettell

Could you pass the silhouettes and frou frou please? I'd like to add them to my palette, thank you! LOL..I have always been a fan of silhouettes and cameos. A few years ago a friend gave me a vintage silhouette book from the 1920's, complete with cut scenes inside, then I picked up a silhouette book in California last year, and recently I discovered one I had been given as a child.

I'm constantly trying to go beyond the limits, trying to create something original or to give my twist on something vintage, to play with, have fun with and silhouettes have allowed me to do just that, PLAY!

From Silhouette Crowns to Silhouette Books, to Silhouette Medallions and Cameo Necklaces, garland, party hats and toppers, I am Silhouette crazed, this insanity led me to my next Silhouette project, The Frou Frou Silhouette Cabinet.

The original piece came from my friend Joyce's Store: Rose Petal Porch www.rosepetalporch.co located across the street from my store: Piddlestixs.

I walked in saw the cabinet, looked at Joyce and she knew, it was going to my store, lol.

My mission, re-paint, eliminate the contact paper inside and frou frou it up.

To start I sanded the piece, then painted the cabinet with Shabby Salmon Color. Next I enhanced the wood braiding and trims with Kettle Black Paint (Yes a paint similar to my last name, LOL), then free hand painted a silhouette image to the front cabinet door.

Creating your own frou frou masterpieces is easier then you think, I included simple project instructions which can be applied to various painted projects.

Materials:
- Blank Canvas, un-finished/old furniture, etc.
- Latex paint in colors of choice (primer and paint all in ones are perfect for these projects)
- Silhouette image sized to dimension of choice or silhouette stencil
- Broken jewelry pieces
- Hardware
- Quick Grip glue or epoxy
- Spray adhesive
- Multi purpose screw driver
- Painters tape
- Sandpaper
- Paint brushes in a few sizes
- Pencil

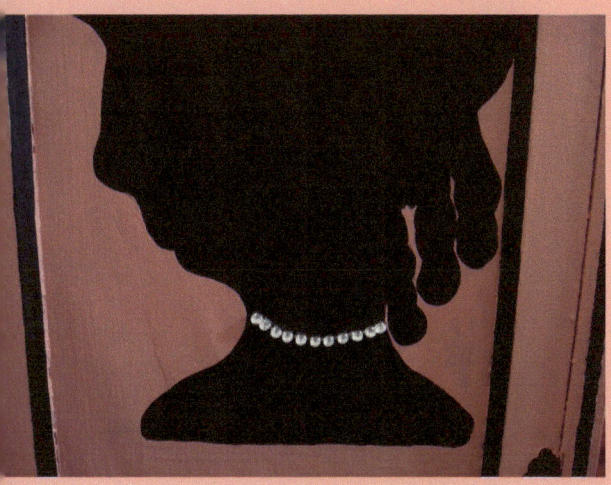

Directions:
1. Sand furniture with sandpaper to remove any film or shine, wipe of sand dust with damp paper towel.
2. Begin painting your sanded furniture with paint of choice, let dry. Apply second coat of paint, let dry.
3. Decide on a silhouette shape or pattern, re-size according to size of your piece, on your computer, print, then cut out.
4. Next spray the spray adhesive to the back of the cut out silhouette, attach to your furniture, trace the cut out with a pencil, remove the cut out silhouette. Now paint the traced silhouette with black paint or color of choice.
5. Enhance parts of your furniture with more black paint or color of choice using a smaller paint brush.
6. Embellish your piece with hardware, broken jewelry and embellishments, using quick grip glue or epoxy.

Tips and Tricks:
- If you aren't too computer savvy bring your silhouette image to your local printer store and have them re-size and print your image.
- If you don't want to paint the silhouette on, decoupage the cut out silhouette onto the furniture using Mod Podge.
- Glue a rhinestone pin to a wooden knob and use as a handle.
- Try fabric or vintage wallpaper as the silhouette image.
- Use a blank canvas instead of furniture or wood scraps.

Here are some pictures of the finished cabinet. The picture on the right shows the piece filled with items, ready for sale at Piddlestixs. I choose to fill the cabinet with frames which are perfect for housing small silhouette images or fun artwork. The top holds jewelry and artful wares.

Artist Spotlight
Marfi Bradford

Come with me and explore the magical world of the amazing Marfi................

1. How did you get started?
I was an imaginative child, my backyard would transform into a haunted house, a sea shell, a gypsy wagon. Dressing up, painting rocks and making clay was an everyday thing.

I still remember adding pebbles and bits of twigs to my pots of tempera paint to see how it would affect my paintings.

At the age of 7 my dream was to grow up and be a gypsy artist and live in a tree house!

2. Biggest influences?
My daughters; my blog friends and to be perfectly honest Lisa Kettell.

3. Favorite themes to work in (circus, storybook, steampunk, etc.)
I love fairytales. If I can create something that takes me into an enchanted forest or a cookie house for a few hours then I'm happy. Fantastical carnival punk is what I like :)

4. How would you describe yourself? (quirky, free spirited, fun, magical, etc.)
I try to find magic in everyday things...I'm a bit of a day dreamer. I can drift off holding a piece of blank canvas, just imagining the possibilities. (Magical, day-dreamy, and impulsive).

5. Where can one contact you to purchase your works?
At the moment you can email me or visit my site, if there's interest in any of the art on my blog www.marfibradford.blogspot.com

Steampunk in Bethlehem

In 1899, after 40 years and several changes, the Bethlehem Steel Company adapted to its new name. In 1904, Charles M. Schwab and Joseph Wharton formed the Bethlehem Steel Corporation with Schwab becoming its first president and chairman of its board of directors.

The Bethlehem Steel Corporation ascended to great prominence in American industry, installing the revolutionary grey rolling mill and producing the first wide-flange structural shapes to be made in America. These shapes were largely responsible for ushering in the age of the skyscraper and establishing Bethlehem Steel as the leading supplier of steel to the construction industry.

In 2001, Bethlehem Steel filed for bankruptcy. In 2003, the company's remnants, including its six massive plants, were acquired by the International Steel Group.

In 2007, the Bethlehem property was sold to Sands BethWorks, and plans to build a casino where the plant once stood were drafted. Construction began in fall 2007; the casino was completed in 2009. Ironically, the casino had difficulty finding structural steel for construction, thanks to a global steel shortage and pressure to build Pennsylvania's tax-generating casinos. 16,000 tons of steel will be needed to build the $600 million complex.

This past December, my friend Mark and I headed out to Bethlehem for the Christkindlmarkt Bethlehem, the annual held in Bethlehem, PA, which was recognized by Travel and Leisure Magazine as one of the top holiday markets in the world, filled with unique artisan finds and holiday specialties. This year the market was held inside PNC Plaza at the Steelstacks, which is an arts & cultural campus in Bethlehem, PA, located at the former site of the Bethlehem Steel plant.

What Mark and I found was a mixture of glitter and grunge, a holiday market set in a fascinating steampunk world filled with industrial magic. I don't know what was more fascinating the turn of the century industrial building remnants or the steamy metal vessels still standing. Walking along side these grand ruins filled me with intrigue, sparked my curiosity and awakened my creativity, ideas were just flowing through me. The pictures I took of my journey that day want to be prints, backgrounds or assemblage bases, they are asking me to write a story and to investigate their story from long ago and bring them back to life. This summer I will be heading back to explore some more and to see all the latest additions to the Steelstacks Campus.

For more information on the former Steelworks, the new Steelstacks Campus, Bethlehem, Historic Bethlehem and the Christkindlmarkt visit these links:

www.christkindlmarkt.org
www.steelstacks.org
www.wikipedia.com
www.artsquest.org
www.bethlehempaonline.com

Materials
- Pocket watch casing
- Medium thickness ball chain
- Owl charm and various small charms
- Watch/clock parts, metal findings
- Small jump rings
- Rhinestones, broken jewelry
- Tools: Needle nose pliers, wire cutter
- Glues: Epoxy glue or quick grip

Directions
1. Open pocket watch casing, begin layering various charms, clock parts and metal findings inside the casing, until you are satisfied with the design. I choose to layer a clock charm first, then a phoenix charm, some mini watch dials, a strand of rhinestones, inside the watch casing, with epoxy g
2. Then I attached an owl charm and more rhinestones to the non-glass side of the pocket watch casing using epoxy g
3. Next, slide your pocket watch piece onto the medium sized ball chain.
4. Finally add some extra some charms to the necklace using small and medium jump rings, charms. Attach and close charms to the necklace using a needle nose plier.
5. Optional, add some rhinestone beads, or broken jewelry to the necklace.

Tips/Tricks
- Epoxy glue dries fast, don't mix until you are happy with your design, then mix and attach your pieces.
- If you are good at soldering, make your own necklace casing using glass, solder tape and solder, fill with your favorite steampunk findings.
- Purchase necklace sized glass shadow boxes and fill, like the above.

To purchase Joan's work visit her at Piddlestixs, our webstore or site:
www.artoperanj.com
MoonfairesWorld/Artfire.com

These Sailors Valentines were inspired by trips to Nantucket, the Vineyard and Sanibel, along with my love for vintage splendor. Each of these pieces were made using recycled materials and many small shells.

Materials

- Fabric scraps
- Fabric stuffing
- Various upholstery trims & tassels
- Ribbons, sequins, broken jewelry
- Vintage images
- Various small and medium shells
- Gold leafing or metallic paint
- DMC embroidery floss, threading
- Glues: epoxy, hot glue, fabri-tac
- Tools: scissors, needle, glue gun, paint brush or foam brush.
- Optional: rhinestones, velvet, buttons

Directions

1. Cut two heart shapes from scraps of fabric, place the two good sides together and stitch leaving a 2 inch opening, turn right side out, then insert stuffing and stitch shut.
2. Now add decorative borders to your heart using upholstery trims and tassels. Simply line your hearts with trim, stitch in place.

For pearl/jewelry borders, stitch the pearl strands to the heart border using upholstery threat or DMC floss.

3. Apply a vintage image to the center of the heart using fabri-tac, let dry.

4. Begin randomly layering various sized shells onto the heart using epoxy glue.

5. Add extra embellishments using various sequins, ribbons and broken jewelry, secure in place with hot glue.

6. For more dazzle and effect, apply gold leafing or metallic paint to some of the shells using a paint or foam brush.

7. Optional, for more security, apply a coat of mod podge over the vintage image.

Optional:
- Use clear caulk in place of epoxy glue or quick grip glue.
- Instead of stitching the hearts together, use hot glue to close your hearts.
- Try fabric transfer images, old badges or fabric patches.
- Use old ties or clothing as your fabric.

Ideas:
- Create sailor valentines as summer beach mementoes, using your seashore finds.
- Make sailor valentine banners from paper, fabric and chipboard. Hang in your studio.
- Turn a frame into a sailors valentine.
- Use an old pillow as your valentine base.
- Make sailor valentine sachets or wands.

Noted History:

A sailor's valentine is a type of antique souvenir, or sentimental gift, originally brought home from a sailor's voyage at sea for his loved one between 1830 and 1890. Sailor valentines are typically octagonal, glass fronted, hinged wooden boxes ranging from 8" to 15" in width, displaying intricate symmetrical designs composed entirely of small sea shells of various colors glued onto a backing. Patterns often feature a centerpiece such a a compass rose or a heart design, hence the name, and in some cases the small shells ar used to spell out a sentimental message.

Although the name seems to suggest that the sailors themselves made these objects, a large number of them originated in the island of Barbados, which was an important seaport during this period.

Visit wikipedia.com for more historical info

I've been creating some projects using my new line of scrapbook papers, this project is a fun and easy one which involves two sheets of my new papers: Dark Plum Grunge and Optometry Rust, paper shapes, zip dry, thin nails, metal brads, bells, trims and more!

Materials
-Dark Plum Grunge Scrapbook Paper, Lisa Kettell Designs
-Optometry Rust Scrapbook Paper, Lisa Kettell Designs
-Creatology Paper Shapes, Robot Style
-Zip Dry, Beacon Adhesives
-Kids Choice Glue, Beacon Adhesives
-Ornate Metal Brads or metal buttons
-Small jingle bells, red color or color of your choice
-Thin nails or silver painted tooth picks w/glued bead on top
-Tinsel, silver chenille stems, dark color sequins
-tools: wire plier, scissors, pencil

Scrapbook Paper, Dark Plum and Optometry Rust

Paper Shapes, Robots

Ornate Metal Brads and Buttons

1. Gather your supplies for the project.
2. Place robot shape towards the edge of the optometry rust paper, covering the whole robot up to the neck of the piece.
3. Trace the shape onto the paper.

Step: Two

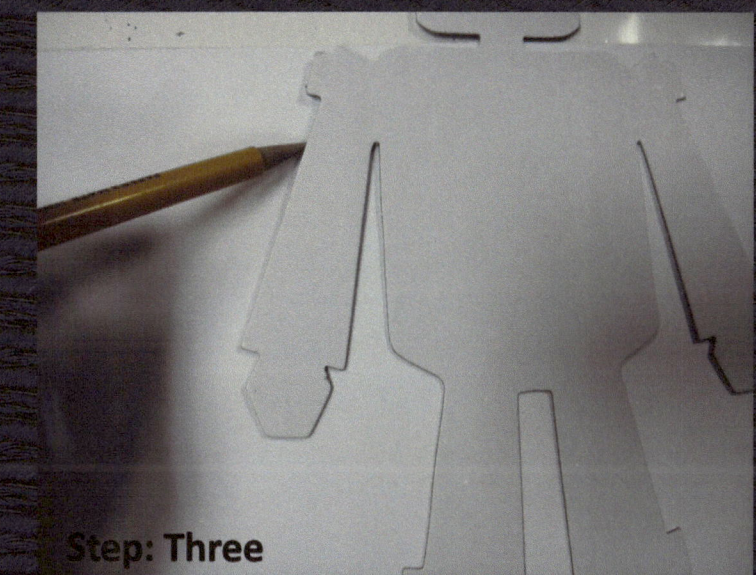
Step: Three

4. Cut out the traced pattern from the paper, set aside. Apply zip dry to the creatology template using your finger, rubbing the glue in with a circular motion.

Step: Four

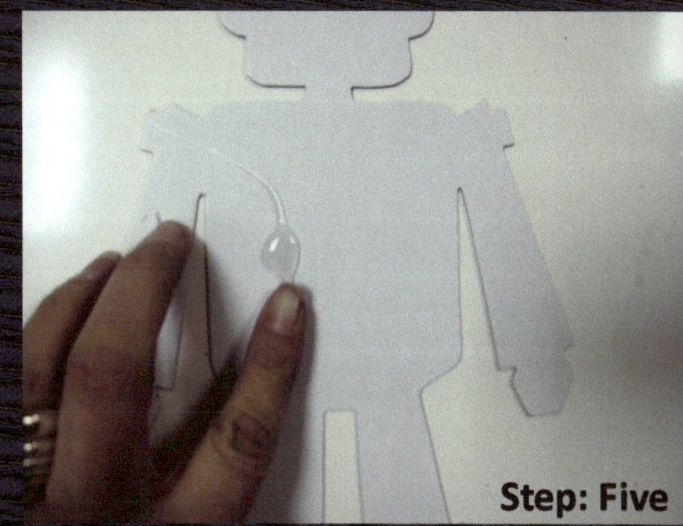
Step: Five

5. Quickly position the cut robot onto the glue lined robot shape, smooth in place. Trace the head shape of the robot onto the Dark Plum Grunge Scrapbook Paper, cut out and glue into place, your piece should now resemble this.

6. Begin embellishing your robot, starting with the face first. Press closed the metal prongs on the back of a brad and the loop of a jingle bell using a wire plier, glue onto the robot for eyes and mouth using Kids Choice glue, now add more metal brads for the robot's buttons, let set for 20 minutes.

Step: Six

Step: Seven

7. Finish embellishing your robot with nails, tinsel, sequin and trims. Add a piece of chenille stem to the back of the robot to turn into an ornament.

Tips/Tricks:
- For extreme steampunk design use quick grip in place of kids choice glue.
- Use washers in place of metal brads.
- Attach a tiny glass vial/bottle to the hand of the robot.
- Add a variety of metal pieces or charms to the whole robot.
- Turn into a ornament for that special boys tree.
- Makes several, add lettering and turn into a room banner
- Turn frou frou robot using the sweet papers in my line.
- Replace robot face with your child's face or friends face.

Pixie Isle! At Night!

Welcome to Grimshaw Alley located in Pixie Isle along the Merwin Sound. Pixie Isle is part of the Pixie Region of Wistica and located 25 miles from land. Since Wistica is south of England, the whole area has many British characteristics.

Pixie Isle is considered a premier seaside destination and famous for the Tri-Sea Pixie Pageant, last years winner was August Platmoore. Lavender, coral powder and moongrass are indigenous to the island. While Wentmoore Holloway made the area famous with his delicious tea called Holloway's Teasers, with flavors such as: Mervander's Twist, Licorice Sunrise and Lavender Vanilla, and many more, which have now been made into scrumptious taffy and candy confections.

Madeline Merwright is pictured here waiting for Percy Spellbinder to start his summer potions class, held every thursday evening at 8pm. $100 pixiepents gets you 8 classes. This is a must do for any young and curious pixie.

Stay tuned for the next installment of Pixie Isle

Meet Kewpie of Fairyland. I have been going above and beyond the jar fairy world, creating fairy and doll vignettes in any glass piece I can find, even in lanterns, candy containers, shadow boxes, vases, bulbs, tea cups, canning jars, and more!

Materials
-Old jar or candy jar
-Paper clay
-Vintage dolly dingle image, Brownies-Palmer Cox image
-Cardstock, lettering
-Millinery: flowers, stamens, floral springs, pearl strands
-Crepe paper rosette
-Shredded pink paper
-Small wood block/square
-Glittered stars, clear glitter, silver glitter
-Acrylic paints: flesh, pink, white, black
-Glue: hot glue, glue stick, craft glue
-Tools: Hot glue gun, scissors

Directions
1. Hand sculpt a kewpie doll head form, then handpaint it, let dry, set aside.
2. Pour craft glue onto the inside bottom of the jar, press shredded pink paper onto the glued base.
3. Using glue stick, layer Dolly Dingle image on cardstock, cut out, hot glue to wood square. Now glue the wood square to the inside base.
3. Add the variety of millinery, glitter stars and Brownies Image into the jar. Add some glitter.
4. Attach the lid, glue a crepe paper rosette to the lid top, hot glue paper clay kewpie head to the center of the roseete, top off with clear glitter.
5. Add lettering or banner, your jar is complete.

Tips/Tricks
-Use a pre-made doll head or part from the Lisa Kettell Designs Line.
-Use paper doll images or family photos in place of Dolly Dingle.

Vintage Paper Doll Collage Sheet